j
582.16
P

9638

Pine, Tillie S.
Trees and how we use them

Trees help us in many wonderful ways. They provide homes for birds, animals, and insects—and food for us all. They shade our homes and streets from the hot, blazing sun and they help prevent floods. How many other ways are trees useful?

In this stimulating new book, Tillie S. Pine and Joseph Levine discuss the importance of the leaf, seeds, bark, trunk, and root as they explore the way trees grow and how they grow, demonstrate how living trees help us in all kinds of weather, and tell of the fruit and nuts and other things we get from trees. They also describe tree farms where baby trees are grown, the way the tree logs are floated to mills, and how boatmakers, violin makers, furniture makers, toy makers, sculptors, paper manufacturers, and others work with various kinds of wood.

With many simple experiments and lively illustrations by Bernice Myers, TREES AND HOW WE USE THEM is an exciting addition to the popular "All Around" series.

TREES
AND HOW WE
USE THEM

by Tillie S. Pine
and Joseph Levine

Illustrated by Bernice Myers

McGRAW-HILL BOOK COMPANY

New York • Toronto • London • Sydney
St. Louis • San Francisco • Mexico • Panama

For Deborah and Caren
who love to watch things grow.

Would you like to know—
   how living trees help us,
   how to find out how old
a tree is,
   what a tree "farm" is,
   why we need forests,
   how tree seeds travel,
   where rubber comes from,
   how trees can keep a house cool,
   how you can grow a tree
in your house,
   how trees help prevent floods,
   why we cut down trees,
   where lumber comes from,
   where maple syrup comes from?
This book answers these
questions. It also tells you
many, many other things about trees
and how we use them.

Visit a lumberyard.
What do you see?
You see stacks and stacks of wood all around
You see—
  long boards, short boards,
  thick boards, thin boards,
  wide boards, narrow boards.
You can also see—
  fancy strips of wood,
  panels and frames,
  dowel sticks, poles, and sawdust.
You may also see the workers cutting
wood and their electric saws!

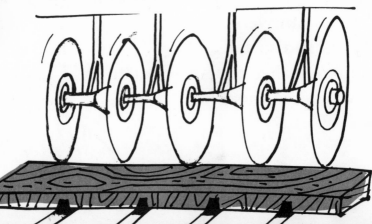

Ask the man to let you touch and hold
some of this wood.

Is it smooth or is it rough?

If you scratch a piece of scrap lumber,
is it hard or is it soft?

Before you leave the lumberyard
ask the man if he would give you some
small pieces of wood, of different kinds,
that he plans to throw away.

Do you know where all this wood
comes from?

It comes from the trees cut down
in forests!

We use these forests in different ways.
We hike through forests
and picnic in them.
We swim in the forest lakes.
We watch the birds and listen
to their beautiful songs.
We look for forest animals
scampering around and climbing trees.
We enjoy the beauty of the thousands
of trees.
And—
forest rangers help us keep forests
safe from harm—especially from fire.

Can you believe that millions of trees
are cut down in these forests every year?

They are!

But—
millions of young trees are planted in their
place to grow into big trees.

Where do these baby trees come from?

Farmers grow them on *tree farms!*

They grow many different kinds
of trees on these farms.

When we need new trees to take
the place of trees cut down, workers get
the young trees from the tree farms
and plant them in fields or forests.

We say they *transplant* them.

In this way, we keep our forests
growing, or we grow new forests.

At Christmastime, tree farmers
cut down Christmas trees and send them
to cities all over the country.

So—people can buy
Christmas trees for their homes year
after year, year after year.

What do lumbermen do with the trees
that are cut down in forests?
They trim the branches, float
the logs down rivers,
and send them on trucks and trains
to different kinds of mills and factories.
In the lumber mills, workers use
huge saws, run by motors, to cut these logs
into boards of different shapes and sizes.
And—
we use this wood in many ways.
You can do things to help
you understand how we use wood.

Look at the pieces of wood that the lumberman gave you.

Put a few pieces of your wood into a tub of water.

What do you see? They float!

Put a small metal spoon into the water.

What happens? It sinks.

Now put the spoon on a floating piece of wood. Does the wood keep the spoon from sinking? Yes, it does.

You found out that wood floats and can carry things on water.

So—
lumbermen can float tree logs down streams to mills,

and—
lumbermen can make wooden rafts to carry things on rivers and lakes.

Now—
saw one of your pieces of wood
into different sizes.

You can nail or glue some of these
pieces together to make a simple picture
frame, a breadboard, or a pair of bookends
    because—
wood can be sawed and fastened together
to make different things.

Who knows this?

Box makers do. They make all kinds of wooden boxes and crates in factories.

We use these boxes and crates to ship fruit, bottles, furniture, and pictures to places near and far.

Furniture makers do. They use wood to make many different kinds of furniture.

Toymakers do. They make many wooden pull toys, blocks, boats, and other toys for boys and girls.

Now do this.

Sandpaper a rough piece of your wood.

What happens? The wood becomes smoother.

Brush a little oil stain on the smooth part of your wood.

What do you see? You see that the color of your wood has changed. You may even see lines in the wood. We call these lines—the *grain* of the wood.

Sandpaper and stain the things you made.

Who else knows that wood can be smoothed and stained?

Furniture makers do. They smooth and stain the furniture they make to show the beautiful colors and grains of the wood.

Sculptors do. They cut and chisel wood to make statues and figures. They smooth and polish the wood.

Look at the wood in your house.
Do you see the different stains and grains?

Now do this.
Do you have a long, narrow, thin
piece of wood in your collection?
Put it on the floor.
Step on one end of this piece.
Lift the other end with your hand.
Does it bend? Yes, it does.
You can make a simple bow from this piece
of wood. You can make an arrow from
another thin piece of wood.
You can have fun shooting
your arrow at a target.

Who knows that some wood can be bent?

Boat builders do. They shape and bend long pieces of wood and fasten them together to make boats.

Violin makers do. They cut, shape, and bend thin pieces of wood to make violins. Some violin makers also make other musical instruments such as cellos and bass viols.

Chair makers do. Sometimes they bend wood to make chairs of different shapes.

People who make diving boards do.
They use long, heavy, strong wood.
They fasten the boards to the
diving platform of a swimming pool.
When you jump up and down on the
free end of a diving board,
you bend the board. This helps
to push you up just before
you dive into the water.

Now do this.
Try to scratch the different pieces
of your wood with your thumbnail.
You see that you can make
scratches in some pieces of your wood
    and—
that you cannot make scratches in
other pieces of your wood.
This is because some kinds of wood
are harder than others.

Now do this.

Put a few drops of water on a piece of your wood.

After a few minutes, what happens?

The wood takes in the water.

We say it *absorbs* the water

and—

the wood stays wet.

Sometimes, wood that is in damp places for a long time takes in water and rots.

Why?

Certain tiny plants grow on this wet wood and eat away the wood.

This makes the wood crumbly.

We say the wood rots,

but—

we know how to help keep wood from rotting.

You can do something to show
yourself what we do.

Brush oil paint on one of the
pieces of your wood.

Rub wax on another piece of your wood.

Let both pieces dry.

Now—put a few drops of water
on each piece.

After a few minutes, what do you see?

The drops of water stay on each piece.
The wood does *not* absorb the water. Why?

The oil paint and the wax keep
the water from getting into the wood.

In this way, we protect the wood
from getting wet.

We also use varnish, special oils,
and chemicals to do this.

In these ways, builders, carpenters,
furniture makers, toy makers, sculptors—
all protect the wood they use.

What else do we get from cut-down trees?
Some of the logs,
cut down in forests,
are sent to special mills.
There they are ground up into small
pieces by huge machines.

These pieces are mixed with water,
glue, starch, and special chemicals.
The mixture is heated and stirred
into a pulp in large vats.

The pulp is poured on big
screens where the water drips through.
The pulp is rolled out and dried.
Then it is cut into long, thin sheets.

These sheets are paper!

Books and magazines,
    newspapers and writing paper,
    tissues and cartons,
    bags and candy wrappers—
all are made of paper.
    Look around you in your house.
Make a list of all the things
you see that are made of paper.

    We use cut-down trees
in another way.
    Do you have a fireplace in
your house?
    If you do, you burn logs from
cut-down trees for the fire.

We get wood from many different kinds of trees.

oak

maple

redwood

pine

cedar

hickory

WHERE DO TREES COME FROM?

As you know, trees are plants that grow from seeds in soil. When the trees grow up, they make their own seeds.

How do these tree seeds get into the soil?

Some seeds travel by air.

These seeds float and spin in the wind until they fall into the soil.

What helps them fall? The gravity pull of the earth does.

hemlock

maple seeds

elm

sycamore seeds

elm seeds

pine cones

Some seeds travel by water.

Some pine cones fall into streams
and float until they wash up on banks.
The shells dry and open up, and the seeds
get into the soil.

Some coconuts fall into the ocean and
float thousands of miles to lands far away.
They wash up on the shores and get
buried in the soil. The hard
shells rot and the seeds
inside begin to sprout.

coconuts

Some seeds are carried
by squirrels and chipmunks.

The animals take the seeds
from the trees for food. They store
some of the seeds in the ground.
They do not dig up all the seeds
they store. The seeds that are
left in the ground grow into
new trees.

Now you know—
trees grow their own seeds,
gravity helps seeds fall down,
seeds travel to different places
in different ways,
    and—
new trees grow from these seeds
in soil.

hickory nuts

acorns

walnuts

You can plant your own
tree seeds indoors.

Get a large pot of soil.

Put two or three grapefruit seeds,
apple seeds, or lemon seeds one inch
under the top of the soil.

Put a little water into the soil
each day. Be very patient. It may
take a month or two,

but—

you will see tiny plants growing
from your seeds.

Take care of your tiny plants and soon
you will see small trees growing. As the
small trees get bigger, you can replant
them into their own large pots of soil.

HOW DO TREES GROW?

What do you see when you look
at a tree?

You see leaves and branches.

You see a trunk.

And—

there is a part you do not see.

This part is in the soil. It is
the roots of the tree.

What do the roots do for the tree?

You know that even strong winds
do not usually push over trees.

Why not?

Trees have many roots. They are
strong and they are spread out
in the soil. They hold the trees firmly
in the ground.

What else do the roots do?

Rain falls on the soil. The many tiny root hairs near the ends of the roots take in some of this water and send it up to all parts of the tree.

What does the trunk do for the tree?

The trunk holds up the branches of the tree.

What else does the trunk do?

You can do something simple to help you understand.

Put some ink into a glass half filled with water.

Make a few cuts in the bottom of a stalk of celery and stand this end in the water.

After a few hours, cut the celery stalk across the center.

Look at the cut edges.

You see spots the color of the ink around the cut edges. These spots really show you where there are thin tubes in the celery.

Now—

cut the celery the long way. You see
the thin tubes clearly.

The colored water comes up
the celery through these tubes.

In the same way, the water
from the roots of a tree goes up the
tree through thin tubes. These tubes
are in the trunk and branches
underneath the hard bark of the tree.

The tubes also reach into the leaves.
And so—
the water gets to all parts of the tree.

What does the bark do for the tree?

The bark is a hard coat that covers
the trunk and branches of the tree.
It helps to protect the tree against
tree-harming insects and tree diseases.
It also keeps the tree
from drying out.

What do the leaves do for the tree?
Take a green leaf from a tree.
Do you see the veins in the leaf?
These veins have many tiny tubes in them.

Break the leaf and feel the broken edge.
It is moist.   This is water that comes
from the roots.

Rub the wet edge on a piece
of white paper.   You see a green
spot on the paper.

There is a special chemical
in the leaf.

We call this chemical—
chlorophyll (KLOR-uh-fil).

It makes the leaf green.

A leaf also has many tiny openings on
its surface.   Air goes into the leaf
through these openings.   The leaf takes
a gas out of this air.

This gas is—*carbon dioxide* (di-AHK-side).

Now do this.

Place a leafy plant on a sunny windowsill.

Place another leafy plant in a closet.

Water both plants.

After several days, look at both plants.

What do you see?

The plant in the sun looks strong and healthy.

The plant in the closet is drooping. Why?

Plants need sunlight to grow.

Trees, too, need sunlight to grow.

So you see—
    leaves have water in them,
    leaves have chlorophyll,
    leaves take in carbon dioxide,
    leaves need sunlight
and—
leaves use all of these things together
to make food for the trees.
    We call this food—*sugar.*
    The leaf is really a sugar "factory."
    Chlorophyll is the "machine."
    Sunlight makes the "machine" work.
    Carbon dioxide and water
are the things the "machine" uses.
    And—
sugar is what is made
in this "factory."

Sugar

Water

What happens to this sugar?
It travels from the leaves
through tubes under the hard bark
of the branches and trunk to all
parts of the tree
and—
all the parts of the tree use this sugar
as food to help the tree grow.
Some of this sugar goes
all the way down to the roots.
Here the sugar is stored for the tree
to use when it needs it.
Now you know—
the roots, the trunk, and the leaves
all work together to help the tree grow.
And—
as the tree grows, it gets taller,
its trunk and branches get thicker,
its roots get larger and stronger.

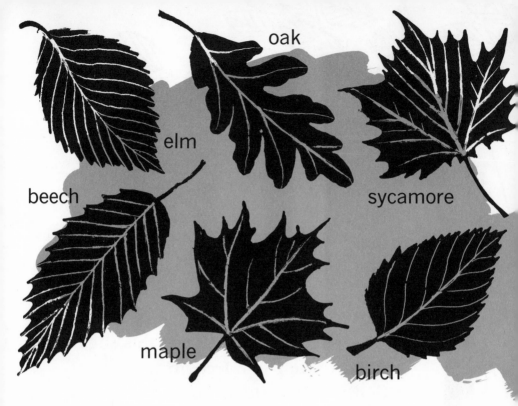

oak

elm

beech

sycamore

maple

birch

Do you live in a place
where the seasons change from warm
to cold every year?
In the autumn, the leaves
of many trees turn from green
to beautiful shades of brown, yellow, or red.
And—
they fall to the ground.
We call the trees that lose
their leaves—
deciduous (dih-sɪj-uh-wus) trees.

You know that some trees
do *not* lose their leaves. We call
these trees—*evergreen* trees.
They have different kinds of leaves.
They stay on the trees and remain
green all year round. We call
them—*needle* leaves.

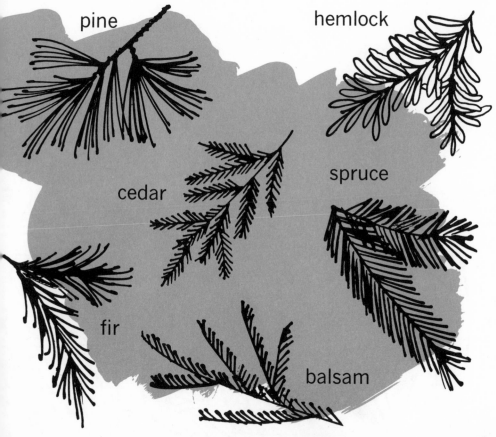

pine

hemlock

cedar

spruce

fir

balsam

Would you be surprised to know
that you can find out how old a tree is?
Walk in a field or a park.
Find a stump of a tree that was cut down.
Look closely at the top of the stump.
Do you see the "rings"?
Each "ring" is really a layer
of new wood that the living tree
grew each year.
So—there is one ring for each year.
In this way, year by year,
the trunk grew thicker.
Now—
count the number of "rings"
you see on the stump.
How old was this tree
when it was cut down?

HOW DO LIVING TREES HELP US?

After a rain, take a walk in the woods.
Look at the ground under the trees,
and—
look at the ground that is not
under the trees.

Is the ground under the trees as wet
as the ground *not* under the trees?

No, it is not.   Why?

The spreading branches and leaves
keep the rain from falling hard on the
ground under the trees,
and—
they keep the rain from washing away
the soil.

In the same way, the trees in the
forest help keep the soil under the
trees from getting too much rain
and washing away the soil.

Walk in the park in the autumn.
See how the fallen leaves cover
the ground like a "carpet."
What does this "carpet" do?
It helps keep the water in the ground.
This keeps the soil from drying out
and blowing away in strong winds.
What happens to this "carpet"?
Dig through the leaves.
Do you see that those underneath
are crumbling into smaller and
smaller pieces?
Slowly, over a long time, the "carpet"
of leaves changes and helps make new soil.
In the forests, too, the "carpet" of fallen
leaves keeps the water in the soil
and—
helps make new rich soil for the trees.

You know that trees take in water
through their roots.

You also know how fallen
leaves help keep water in the ground.

But—
what happens when very heavy
rains fall and mountain snows melt?

There is water—so much water
that it can cause a flood!

But—
the thousands and thousands
of trees in the forest—

and—
the thick carpet of the forest
floor both hold water—so
much water that it often
can help to prevent a flood!

HOW DO LIVING TREES HELP?

How do these trees help
keep the house cool?

How do birds use these trees?

What kind of homes do bees
and squirrels have in these trees?

Why do we plant trees
on city streets?

WHAT DO WE TAKE FROM LIVING TREES?

Have you ever wondered
where the maple syrup comes from
that you pour over your pancakes?

In the early spring, when snow
is still on the ground, the farmer
carefully drills holes in the trunks
of sugar maple trees.

We say he "taps" the trees.
This tapping does not harm the trees.

The farmer hangs buckets
below the holes. Drop by drop,
a liquid drips out into the buckets.

The liquid is some of the food
that the roots are beginning
to send up into the trees.

We call this liquid—*maple sap.*

This sap has maple sugar in it.

It also has much water in it.   The farmer gathers the sap and boils it in large pots.

You can do something simple to show yourself why he boils the sap.

Put two tablespoons of sugar into half a glass of warm water.

Stir the sugar until it "disappears."

The sugar dissolves in the water.

Now pour this sugar water into a small saucepan.

Boil the water slowly.

As the water boils, you see that it begins to get thicker.

Turn off the heat.

Why does the sugar water thicken?

Some of the water disappears into the air.   It evaporates.

And—

the sugar water thickens.

In the same way, when
the farmer boils the maple sap,
some of the water evaporates.
    The sap that is left in the pot
is the maple syrup you pour over your pancakes.
    Sometimes, the farmer boils off
more of the water
    and—
what is left in the pot is—*maple sugar.*

What else do we take from living trees?
Do you have a rubber ball?
Bounce it!
Do you have a rubber band?
Stretch it!
Do you know where the rubber
in these things comes from?
It comes from trees.

In hot places of South America
and Asia, rubber trees are grown on
farms.

Farmers make careful slashes in the
bark of living rubber trees.
This slashing, too, does not
harm the trees.

The farmers hang cups
below the slashes they make.
A white juice, called *latex,*
oozes out into the cups.
This is liquid rubber.

Workers boil this liquid in large metal pots over hot fires until the liquid becomes solid rubber.

Workers in factories sometimes use other materials to make a different kind of rubber—man-made rubber.

Who uses rubber?

Tire makers do—when they make tires for cars, trucks, and bicycles.

Toy makers do—when they make rubber balls, balloons, and other toys.

Other factory workers do—when they make mats, drain boards, foam rubber for cushions and mattresses, rubber bands, erasers, and covering for electric wires.

How many things can you find in your home that have rubber in them?

There is another kind of juice that we take from trees such as the *acacia* (uh-KAY-sha) and the *eucalyptus* (you-kuh-LIP-tus) trees.

We call this juice—*gum.*

This gum is sometimes used to make—

floor polish and shoe polish,
paints, varnishes, and stains,
soaps, waxes, crayons,
drugs, bug powder, perfume,
and—

the gum from the *sapodilla* (sap-uh-DILL-uh) tree, which grows in hot climates, is used to help make— *chewing gum!*

What else do we take from living trees?

Do you know any other fruits
and nuts that grow on trees?

We get something else from living trees!

You found out that leaves take in air and that they take carbon dioxide from this air to make sugar for the trees.

As they make this sugar, the leaves give off gas, called *oxygen* (AHK-si-jun).

The leaves give off this oxygen into the air

and—

people, animals, birds, insects—
all breathe in air that has the oxygen they need to live.

Now you know that we get many different kinds of things from living trees and from cut-down trees.

Scientists all over the world are trying to discover still other ways of using trees to make new things for people.

Do you think you would like to be one of these tree scientists when you grow up?

About the Authors and Artist

Tillie S. Pine and Joseph Levine are co-authors of the "All Around" series, which now includes TREES AND HOW WE USE THEM. Their second group of science and history books—THE INDIANS KNEW, THE PILGRIMS KNEW, THE CHINESE KNEW, THE ESKIMOS KNEW, THE EGYPTIANS KNEW and THE AFRICANS KNEW —has been universally accepted.

Mrs. Pine, a teacher for many years, was on the staff of the Bank Street College Workshop. Mr. Levine, a former science teacher, is principal of P.S. 48, Bronx, New York.

Bernice Myers has illustrated nine of the "All Around" books as well as UNDERSTANDING FOOD by Beulah Tannenbaum and Myra Stillman, OFF INTO SPACE! by Margaret O. Hyde, and WHAT MAKES IT GO? by Rose Wyler. During her three years in Paris, she wrote and illustrated several books for Hachette—MOUSTACHE, LES CHATS, MUSICIENS, LE FACTEUR, and OLIVER.